I0065617

The Money Guardian

"Where Tax Strategy Meets Legacy Protection"

©2025, Michael A. Carney

All rights reserved. This book or any portion thereof may not be reproduced or used in any manner whatsoever without the express written permission of the publisher except for the use of brief quotations in a book review.

ISBN: 979-8-99367-770-5

THE MONEY GUARDIAN

By Michael A. Carney

Dedication

To my children — Shamara and Mycah —

This book, and the way I live, are both built around the principle of generational wealth.

Not just in dollars, but in discipline, vision, wisdom, and responsibility.

Not only in assets, but in identity, faith, and knowledge.

"True inheritance is not measured by what you leave for your children — it's measured by what you leave in them."

This book is my investment into you.

My blueprint.

My letter of love.

My legacy.

May it guide you, grow you, and remind you that you come from wealth — not just material, but mental, spiritual, and intentional.

— Dad

Table of Contents

Preface

This Isn't Just a Book. It's a Movement.

I didn't write this book because I wanted to be an author.

I wrote this book because I've sat across from too many hard-working people — entrepreneurs, real estate investors, corporate professionals, heads of households — who've done everything right financially, only to find out they've been playing the wrong game.

They made money.

They paid taxes.

They built businesses.

They raised children.

They followed the rules.

But no one ever handed them the real blueprint — the one the wealthy have used for generations to not only protect their assets, but to build structures that ensure their wealth outlives them.

And every time I showed them how family trusts, strategic business structuring, and IRS-compliant tax mitigation could reduce their liability, maximize their growth, and ensure their children's future — I got the same two questions:

"Is this legal?"

"If this is so powerful, why isn't everyone doing it?"

This book is my answer.

Yes — it's legal. In fact, it's codified into the tax code, trust law, and estate planning systems used by the wealthy, the ultra-wealthy, and nearly every major corporation in America.

And no — everyone's not doing it. Not because they can't, but because they don't know it exists.

WHO THIS BOOK IS FOR

This book is written for people like me — and maybe people like you:

- First-generation wealth builders

- Entrepreneurs trying to shield themselves from taxes and liability

- Parents who want to pass down more than a house and a bank account

- Families recovering from financial trauma

- Business owners sick of watching their income drained by taxes

- High earners trying to figure out where all the money went

- Pastors, teachers, veterans, nurses — people who give everything and retire with too little

Whether you're earning six figures or just getting started, this book will show you what to do next.

WHY IT MATTERS

There's a difference between having money... and being in position.

Being in position means:

- Your assets are protected
- Your taxes are minimized
- Your income is structured smartly
- Your insurance works like a wealth vehicle
- Your children are educated on money
- Your legacy is documented and funded
- Your family doesn't have to guess what happens next

I've seen lives change overnight once these systems are put in place.

That's why I built Acuracounts, Inc., launched Trust University, and created the Blueprint Trust System™ — to bring these tools to the families, earners, and communities that have always deserved better.

This book is the starter key to all of that.

1 — Awakening: Seeing Where You Really Are

"You can't master what you refuse to measure."

THE MOMENT THE CURTAIN PULLED BACK

There's a moment in every person's financial journey when the noise quiets and reality steps into focus.

For me, that moment happened years ago while sitting across from a client—a husband and wife, both exhausted, both convinced they were "doing fine."

They owned a home, drove decent cars, and earned well into six figures.

But when I asked a simple question— *"Do you know what your money is actually doing?"*—their eyes dropped to the table.

They didn't.

That moment changed them.

And it shaped the philosophy that became **The Money Guardian Blueprint™**.

Most people aren't broke because they lack income.

They're broke because they lack *clarity*.

They move through life reacting to bills, chasing paychecks, measuring success by cash flow instead of control.

Awakening begins when you stop guessing—and start knowing.

WHY AWARENESS COMES BEFORE WEALTH

You can't protect what you can't see, and you can't grow what you don't measure.

Every trust, every strategy, every tax advantage we'll discuss later in this book only works if you first know exactly where you stand.

Think of awareness as turning on the lights in a dark room.

You don't suddenly get richer—but you *see* what's really there.

You see the opportunities, the waste, and the patterns that have been silently robbing you.

When I meet with families, I ask five grounding questions:

1. What is your *net worth* right now—assets minus liabilities?

2. How much *interest* did you pay last year versus earn?

3. Where is your *cash actually stored*—and whose name is it under?

4. What would happen to your family if you didn't wake up tomorrow?

5. What is your *financial mission statement*?

If you can't answer those today, don't panic.

This chapter exists to get you there.

THE ILLUSION OF "DOING FINE"

I've sat with physicians who make $400,000 a year and can't save $10,000.

I've met teachers who've never earned six figures but have more stability than executives.

The difference isn't income; it's awareness.

When you're unaware, you operate on financial autopilot:

- You swipe instead of plan.
- You sign instead of read.
- You pay taxes instead of strategize.
- You hope instead of calculate.

Hope is not a wealth plan.

The first act of stewardship is honesty—looking your numbers in the eye, even when they sting.

CREATING YOUR FINANCIAL MIRROR

Grab a notebook, spreadsheet, or the worksheet in your companion guide.

We're going to build what I call the **Financial Mirror**—a snapshot of your real financial life.

1. **List every income source**

   Salary, business revenue, side hustles, investment dividends, rental income.

2. **List every expense**

   Start with fixed (mortgage, insurance, utilities), then variable (food, fuel, entertainment).

3. **List every debt**

   Include balances, interest rates, and minimum payments.

4. **List every asset**

   Bank accounts, vehicles, properties, retirement funds, and any trust assets.

5. **Calculate your Net Worth**

   Assets – Liabilities = Net Worth.

This isn't about judgment—it's about *truth*.

Once you see it, you can measure progress and build protection around it.

AWARENESS REVEALS LEAKS

When clients complete their Financial Mirror, the same surprises appear:

- Forgotten subscriptions.

- Unused insurance policies.

- Debt interest exceeding investment returns.

- Cash sitting idle while inflation eats it alive.

Awareness turns confusion into data, and data into decisions.

From here, you'll begin to identify your **investable surplus**—money you didn't know was leaking out of your life.

That surplus is the seed capital for your trust, your insurance strategies, and your long-term growth vehicles.

MINDSET SHIFT: FROM SURVIVAL TO STRUCTURE

Most of us were taught to "work hard and save money."

No one taught us to *structure* it.

But wealth without structure collapses under pressure—taxes, lawsuits, or even emotion.

Awakening means understanding that money is not moral or emotional; it's mathematical and structural.

When you give every dollar a defined role and location—business account, trust account, reserve fund—you move from survival to strategy.

THE AWARENESS AUDIT

Here's your first Money Guardian™ assignment.

Before the next chapter, perform a **90-Day Awareness Audit**:

- Track every transaction for the next 90 days.

- Categorize each as *essential, lifestyle,* or *leak.*

- At the end, total the leaks.

You'll likely find 10–30 percent of your income hiding in plain sight.

That discovery alone can fund your trust or your first Indexed Universal Life policy.

AWAKENING IS SPIRITUAL TOO

Financial awareness isn't just arithmetic—it's stewardship.

It's saying, "Everything in my care has a purpose."

When you steward well, you invite multiplication.

That's why this journey begins here, with awakening.

As Proverbs 27:23 reminds us:

"Be diligent to know the state of your flocks, and attend to your herds."

In modern terms: *Know your numbers.*

SUMMARY — WHAT AWAKENING GIVES YOU

- **Clarity:** You see where you truly stand.
- **Control:** You direct your cash flow instead of reacting to it.
- **Confidence:** You make decisions from data, not fear.
- **Capacity:** You discover resources to fund protection and growth.

Awareness is the foundation.

Protection is the next wall.

Growth is the roof.

Knowledge and Legacy furnish the home.

In the next chapter, we'll build upon this awakening and design the systems that keep your newfound awareness organized and permanent.

2 — Financial Awareness: Turning Clarity into Strategy

"Money without direction is like water without a container — it seeps away."

FROM SEEING TO STEERING

In Chapter 1, we flipped on the lights.

You saw where your money actually lives, how it moves, and maybe how it leaks.

Now it's time to steer it.

Awareness is insight; strategy is action.

When I coach families, I tell them:

> "If you can tell me exactly where every dollar goes, I can tell you how to build wealth in five years.

If you can't, you'll spend the next twenty trying to figure out where it went."

Financial awareness means converting numbers into navigation.

It's how you stop drifting and start driving.

THE ANATOMY OF CASH FLOW

Most people manage their finances like a garden hose — open the faucet, hope the water lands where it's needed.

We're going to install irrigation.

Think of your cash flow as a living system with five channels:

1. **Operations (Needs):** housing, food, insurance, transportation.

2. **Lifestyle (Wants):** entertainment, travel, upgrades, convenience.

3. **Debt Service:** loans, cards, mortgages.

4. **Growth:** investing, business capital, IUL premiums, education.

5. **Protection:** emergency funds, insurance, and your future trust.

Every dollar you earn must be assigned to a channel *before* it hits your checking account.

That's control.

THE BLUEPRINT BUDGET

I don't use the word *budget* the way traditional planners do.

A budget feels restrictive; a Blueprint Budget feels architectural — it builds something.

Here's the framework I teach clients called the **60-20-10-10 Model**:

Category	Purpose	Example
60 % – Living & Operations	Core expenses	Rent, food, utilities
20 % – Growth & Investment	Money that multiplies	IUL, real estate, business
10 % – Protection & Emergency	Peace-of-mind fund	Savings, insurance
10 % – Purpose & Philanthropy	Values in motion	Giving, tithes, causes

It's simple, flexible, and scalable.

Whether you earn $50K or $500K, this model allocates purpose to every dollar.

TURNING DATA INTO DECISIONS

After you've tracked 90 days of spending, patterns appear.

The next step is what I call the **Awareness Conversion** — turning that raw data into clear directives.

1. **Eliminate leaks** → cancel, consolidate, or automate.

2. **Reclassify expenses** → move lifestyle habits into scheduled "fun accounts."

3. **Automate investing** → treat your trust, IUL, or brokerage like a monthly bill.

4. **Time-block money management** → 30 minutes a week to review and redirect.

You'll be shocked how small tweaks reclaim thousands.

THE POWER OF THE SURPLUS

Financial freedom doesn't start with millions; it starts with surplus — the leftover fuel you redirect toward growth.

I once worked with a nurse earning $82,000 a year.

After her Awareness Audit, we uncovered $1,100 per month in leaks: unused subscriptions, inflated insurance premiums, and impulse buys.

We redirected that $1,100 into a trust-owned IUL policy.

Within four years, it held over $60,000 in cash value — tax-free and compounding.

Awareness funds wealth.

ORGANIZING YOUR FINANCIAL LIFE

To keep clarity permanent, you must build a system — a financial operating model.

Here's the one I use and teach:

- **Account 1 – Operations Account:**

  All income deposits here. It's your financial hub.

- **Account 2 – Growth Account:**

  A separate account (or trust account) for investments and IUL premiums.

- **Account 3 – Emergency & Protection Fund:**

  Three-to-six months of core expenses; never co-mingled with operations.

- **Account 4 – Purpose Account:**

  A giving or family-impact fund to keep your values alive.

This structure mirrors what your trust will eventually formalize — clear, directed flow.

USING TECHNOLOGY AS A TOOL, NOT A TRAP

Apps and dashboards are great — but they can also overwhelm.

Choose one platform (like Monarch, YNAB, or QuickBooks Self-Employed) and commit.

Remember: *software doesn't create discipline; it amplifies it.*

The goal isn't to stare at graphs; it's to gain insight that leads to action.

FAMILY FINANCIAL MEETINGS

One of the best habits I've seen families build is the **Monthly Money Meeting.**

Here's how it works:

- Schedule 60 minutes each month.

- Review income, expenses, goals, and upcoming needs.

- Celebrate wins — paid-off debts, increased savings, smart purchases.

- Teach your children one new money concept each meeting.

When you normalize wealth conversations at home, you re-wire your family tree.

AWARENESS AND TAXES

Here's where awareness meets the IRS.

When you know exactly where your money goes, you can classify it strategically.

Business expenses, charitable contributions, and trust funding each carry tax consequences.

Example: If your trust owns your business or your insurance policy, awareness lets you allocate funds legally and efficiently — reducing taxable income while increasing control.

We'll unpack that in detail in Chapter 9, but it starts with organization.

THE AWARENESS MINDSET

Financial awareness isn't about shame; it's about stewardship.

Every number tells a story: how you value time, security, and purpose.

The goal isn't perfection; it's progress — steady, intentional refinement.

When you look at your accounts and say, *"I know exactly what's happening here,"* you've crossed the first major threshold toward generational wealth.

MONEY GUARDIAN ACTION PLAN

Before moving to Chapter 3, complete these four steps:

1. **Download your last three months of bank and credit-card statements.**

2. **Categorize every transaction** using the 60-20-10-10 model.

3. **Highlight your leaks.**

4. **Automate transfers** to your Growth, Protection, and Purpose accounts.

Do this once, and you'll feel relief.

Do it monthly, and you'll feel control.

Do it yearly, and you'll build wealth.

SUMMARY — AWARENESS IN MOTION

- Awareness without action is stagnation.

- Structure turns clarity into momentum.

- Surplus funding creates the engine of wealth.

- Repetition makes it automatic.

In the next chapter, we'll secure what you've just organized.

Because clarity is powerful — but protection makes it permanent.

3 — Protection & Trust: Locking Down Your Wealth

"Wealth is not what you earn — it's what you keep and protect."

THE TURNING POINT

By the time most people find me, they've already built something — a business, a home, a portfolio, or at least the beginnings of one.

But what they *haven't* built is a fortress around it.

I've seen entrepreneurs make six figures, lose a lawsuit, and end up starting from scratch.

I've seen families lose property to probate court because of one missing document.

I've seen decades of effort evaporate in a single judgment — all because there was no structure.

That's why protection isn't optional.

It's the second foundation of wealth, and the cornerstone of the **Blueprint Trust™**.

PROTECTION VS. PRESERVATION

When I say "protection," I'm not talking about just having insurance or saving money.

Protection means *structuring ownership* — making sure your assets are legally separated from your personal identity.

Because here's the truth:

Anything in your *name* is vulnerable.

Anything in your *structure* is shielded.

Protection is the difference between owning everything and controlling everything.

The wealthy understand this distinction intuitively.

Most people never learn it.

THE LAYERS OF FINANCIAL PROTECTION

Think of protection as a three-layer system:

1. **Legal Layer:** Your entities — trusts, LLCs, corporations.

2. **Insurance Layer:** Your policies — life, disability, liability.

3. **Strategic Layer:** How you integrate and control those tools.

If you only have one layer, you're exposed.

But when all three work together, your wealth becomes nearly untouchable.

REVOCABLE VS. IRREVOCABLE TRUSTS — THE CORE DIFFERENCE

Let's break down what most estate planners never explain clearly.

Type	Key Feature	Control	Protection	Tax Treatment	Use Case
Revocable Living Trust	Can be changed or revoked at anytime	Full control	Minimal	Grantor trust (uses your SSN)	Probate avoidance, basic estate planning
Irrevocable Trust	Permanent once funded	Limited	Strong	Non-grantor (separate EIN)	Asset protection, tax strategy, legacy planning

A **Revocable Living Trust** is an excellent start — it avoids probate and provides continuity.

But for true wealth defense, you need the structure of an **Irrevocable Trust**.

When properly written, an irrevocable trust separates *you* from *your assets* legally — meaning lawsuits, creditors, and even certain taxes can't reach them.

THE BLUEPRINT TRUST™ — THE HYBRID FORTRESS

The **Blueprint Trust™** takes this to another level.

It blends the best of both worlds — the flexibility of a revocable trust with the separation of an irrevocable trust.

Here's how it's classified:

Irrevocable. Discretionary. Complex. Non-Grantor.

Each of those words has power:

- **Irrevocable:** Assets inside can't be pulled back into your name at will. That's what makes them untouchable.

- **Discretionary:** The trustee (you or your successor) controls how and when distributions happen, not the beneficiaries.

- **Complex:** The trust can own multiple asset types — real estate, businesses, insurance, even intellectual property.

- **Non-Grantor:** The trust, not you, is the taxpayer. That distinction opens up IRS-approved strategies that reduce or defer taxation.

"OWN NOTHING. CONTROL EVERYTHING."

John D. Rockefeller, one of history's wealth architects, famously said,

> "Own nothing, control everything."

He wasn't hiding assets out of greed. He was insulating them out of wisdom.

Here's what that means in practice:

- The **trust** owns your business, not you.

- The **trust** owns your real estate, not you.

- The **trust** owns your insurance policies, not you.

Yet you still *control* the trust — as trustee, as manager, as architect.

You've legally separated ownership from control.

That's the key to protection.

HOW LAWSUITS ARE NEUTRALIZED

Let's look at a real example (names changed for privacy).

CASE STUDY: THE JACKSON FAMILY

The Jacksons owned four rental properties in their own names.

A tenant slipped and fell on one property and filed a lawsuit for $600,000.

Their insurance covered $300,000. The rest was exposed.

If they had done nothing, their savings, home equity, and wages could've been seized.

Instead, we restructured:

Each property was transferred into its own **LLC**, and each LLC was then **owned by the Blueprint Trust.**

Now, if a tenant sues one property, the damage stops there.

The other properties — and the family's personal wealth — remain protected.

The lawsuit settled for the insurance limit. The trust stayed intact.

That's how structure beats chaos.

TRUST + ENTITIES = FINANCIAL FIREWALL

The Blueprint Trust doesn't stand alone — it works best when combined with **business entities** like LLCs or corporations.

Here's the basic model:

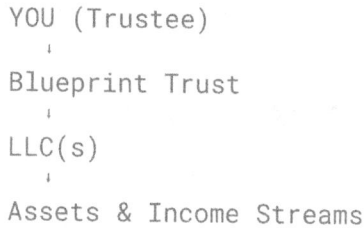

```
YOU (Trustee)
    |
Blueprint Trust
    |
LLC(s)
    |
Assets & Income Streams
```

Each level adds a wall between you and liability.

If someone sues your business, they hit the LLC — not you.

If they pierce the LLC, they meet the trust — and stop there.

This is how you *layer* protection: legally, not emotionally.

INSURANCE AS PROTECTION, NOT REACTION

Most people buy insurance reactively — car, home, life — because someone told them to.

But inside a Blueprint System, insurance becomes strategic.

Life Insurance (IUL or Whole Life):

When owned by your trust, the payout bypasses probate and funds your legacy tax-free.

Umbrella Liability Coverage:

Protects against large claims that exceed your primary policies.

Disability & Long-Term Care:

Prevents income loss from becoming a financial crisis.

Key-Man Insurance:

For business owners — protects the company if a crucial person dies or becomes disabled.

Insurance fills the gaps between legal layers — it's not your defense, it's your cushion.

AVOIDING PROBATE — THE SILENT WEALTH KILLER

Probate is public, slow, and expensive.

It's the government's way of redistributing your assets under court supervision.

Without a trust, your estate could spend 6–24 months tied up in court, with legal fees eating up 5–10% of its value.

During that time, your family can't touch your assets — even for funeral costs or mortgage payments.

With a funded trust, your assets bypass court entirely.

They pass directly, privately, and immediately.

That's not a theory. That's design.

CHOOSING YOUR TRUSTEE WISELY

The most critical person in this system is the **Trustee** — the one who carries your intentions forward.

You can serve as the initial trustee while living, but you must name a **successor trustee** to step in when needed.

Choose someone with:

- Integrity and judgment

- Basic financial literacy

- Willingness to follow the rules you've written

And remember: *you can separate roles.*

One person can manage finances; another can handle family matters.

That balance keeps emotion

PROTECTION IN PRACTICE

When clients complete their protection phase, I walk them through a "Protection Map."

Here's what it looks like:

Category	Owned By	Protected By
Primary Residence	Trust	Insurance + Legal Title
Business	LLC (owned by trust)	Operating Agreement
Rental Properties	Separate LLCs	Insurance + Trust
Vehicles	Personal or Business	Insurance
Life Insurance	Trust	Tax-Free Legacy
Bank Accounts	Trust	FDIC + Legal Control

Every asset has a home. Every risk has a wall. Every dollar has direction.

That's protection in motion.

MONEY GUARDIAN™ ASSIGNMENT

Before the next chapter, complete your **Protection Checklist**:

1. Review your current ownership titles. Whose name is really on them?

2. Identify which assets belong inside your future trust.

3. Research umbrella liability insurance for your household and business.

4. Choose at least one person who could serve as your successor trustee.

5. Write down your "why" — the reason you want your wealth protected.

You're not doing this to hide from the world.

You're doing it to protect the world you're building.

SUMMARY — FORTIFY BEFORE YOU MULTIPLY

- Protection comes before growth.

- Lawsuits, taxes, and probate are predictable — plan, don't react.

- Structure equals security.

- Trusts and entities create legal distance.

- Insurance fills the financial gaps.

When your wealth is shielded, your future becomes unstoppable.

In the next chapter, we'll take the protection you've built and ignite it — turning your structure into a growth engine that multiplies your money while keeping it safe.

4 — Growth & Acceleration: Making Your Money Work Twice

"Don't work for money — make money work for you, twice."

FROM DEFENSE TO OFFENSE

If protection is your financial fortress, then growth is your army.

It's the moment you stop guarding what you have and start multiplying it.

After helping hundreds of families build their trusts and restructure their income, I've learned this:

Once people feel protected, they finally give themselves permission to grow.

Fear fades, clarity sharpens, and creativity awakens.

That's the shift from surviving to thriving.

THE TRUE MEANING OF GROWTH

Growth isn't about chasing the next big investment.

It's not about gambling on crypto, or buying five rental properties because someone said "real estate never loses."

Growth is about intentional expansion — multiplying what you already have through structure, timing, and intelligent leverage.

When your Blueprint Trust is in place, growth no longer depends on hustle.

It depends on systems.

You're not just making more money — you're making *smarter money*.

THE FOUR PATHS OF GROWTH

Every financial ecosystem expands in four primary ways.

1. **Compounding:**

   Earning interest on your interest — the quiet, consistent force that turns thousands into millions over time.

2. **Leverage:**

   Using other people's money (or institutions') to accelerate your own outcomes.

3. **Tax Strategy:**

   Legally reducing what leaves your hands so more stays to grow.

4. **Structure:**

   Positioning assets under entities and trusts to amplify protection and flexibility.

When you align these four, you enter what I call **The Wealth Flywheel** — growth that sustains itself even when you stop working.

DOUBLE-DUTY DOLLARS —
THE SECRET OF THE WEALTHY

One of the most powerful lessons I teach is the **double-duty dollar** concept.

Most people only earn interest in one place: a savings account, a 401(k), or a single investment.

The wealthy earn interest twice on the *same dollar.*

Here's how:

They deposit their money into a **trust-owned Indexed Universal Life (IUL) policy.**

That money compounds tax-deferred inside the policy — earning 5–9% annual average returns depending on the index.

Then, instead of withdrawing it, they **borrow against it** — using the insurance company's money — while their original funds continue compounding untouched.

They use the borrowed funds to:

- Invest in real estate

- Fund business growth

- Lend to their own trust-owned LLCs

Now the same dollar earns in *two places at once:*

Inside the IUL, and inside the investment.

That's smart money.

CASE STUDY: SAMANTHA'S FINANCIAL BREAKTHROUGH

Samantha was a real estate agent earning about $175,000 a year.

She had no retirement plan and was paying heavy taxes as a sole proprietor.

We restructured her income flow:

- Created an LLC for her commissions

- Made the Blueprint Trust the sole member of the LLC

- Established a trust-owned IUL policy

- Redirected her business profit (after expenses) into the policy

Then, using policy loans, the trust funded a duplex purchase — held under a separate LLC also owned by the trust.

Her duplex now generates $2,200 a month in rent, and her IUL continues compounding tax-free.

That's growth by design — not luck.

HOW THE IRS HELPS YOU GROW (IF YOU KNOW HOW)

Here's something most people never hear from their accountant:

The IRS will pay *you* interest.

If you've overpaid taxes in prior years — and many self-employed professionals have — you can amend your returns for the past three years.

When your Blueprint Trust reorganizes your income properly, the IRS owes you refunds *plus interest* (usually 4–7% compounded).

You're literally reclaiming capital from the past to fund your future.

It's not magic-it's mathematics, written into the tax code.

THE FLOW OF GROWTH — TRUST AS FINANCIAL HEADQUARTERS

When structured correctly, your Blueprint Trust becomes the financial headquarters for your wealth.

Here's what the flow looks like:

```
Business Income (LLC or S-Corp)

       ı

Operating Expenses Paid

       ı

Net Profit to Blueprint Trust

       ı

Trust Allocations:
    • Growth Account (IUL, real estate, investments)
    • Protection Account (insurance, reserves)
    • Purpose Account (giving, education)
```

This is how the wealthy operate.

It's why money seems to flow to them effortlessly — they've built pipelines, not puddles.

LEVERAGE WITHOUT RISK

The word "leverage" scares people because they associate it with debt.

But good leverage is different — it's *strategic borrowing against appreciating assets.*

When your trust owns a property or policy, and that asset grows in value, you can borrow against it without triggering a taxable event.

You still control the asset, you still earn on it, and you gain liquidity.

That's how you fund new opportunities without touching your principle — a cornerstone of infinite banking and trust-based growth.

THE RULE OF 72 — THE SPEED OF WEALTH

Let's talk compounding math.

The **Rule of 72** is a simple way to estimate how long it takes your money to double.

Take 72 and divide it by your annual rate of return.

Rate	Years to Double	Example
4%	18 years	Traditional savings
8%	9 years	Trust-owned IUL
12%	6 years	Private lending or real estate

When your structure consistently earns 8–12%, your wealth doubles every 6–9 years — *without* working longer hours.

That's acceleration.

REINVESTING THE SURPLUS

Growth thrives on momentum.

Once your awareness (from Chapter 2) produces surplus, reinvest it through the Blueprint channels:

1. **Trust-Owned Investments:** Real estate, private equity, or lending.

2. **Insurance Vehicles:** IUL or whole life for compounding and liquidity.

3. **Education:** Courses, certifications, and family learning (Chapter 5).

4. **Philanthropy:** Giving that creates impact *and* tax deductions.

Your goal is to have *every dollar* performing two or more functions — earning, protecting, educating, or giving.

AVOIDING GROWTH TRAPS

Growth without discipline becomes chaos.

Here are the three traps that derail most people:

1. **Lifestyle Creep:** As income rises, so do expenses. Counter this with automation.

2. **Chasing Returns:** Don't confuse motion with progress. Stick to structure.

3. **Neglecting Taxes:** Always integrate growth with your CPA or tax strategist — never in isolation.

Smart growth is sustainable growth.

THE MONEY GUARDIAN™ GROWTH PLAN

Before moving forward, complete this short plan:

1. **Identify Your Growth Vehicle:** Choose one — IUL, real estate, business, or education.

2. **Set Your Compounding Goal:** How fast do you want your wealth to double?

3. **Automate Contributions:** Treat investments like mandatory bills.

4. **Track ROI Quarterly:** Review performance in your trust's financial meeting.

5. **Reinvest Profits:** Growth must feed itself — not lifestyle.

SUMMARY — MULTIPLICATION THROUGH DESIGN

- Growth starts when protection gives you permission to expand.

- The Blueprint Trust converts income into compounding wealth.

- Double-duty dollars let one asset earn twice.

- Tax refunds, leverage, and structure accelerate progress.

- Every dollar must perform — or be reassigned.

You've built awareness. You've installed protection. You've ignited growth.

Now it's time to ensure your family keeps the wisdom that sustains it.

5 — Knowledge & Financial Literacy: The Missing Inheritance

"It's not what you leave to your children that matters most — it's what you leave in them."

THE FORGOTTEN CURRENCY

I've sat across from families worth millions — portfolios, properties, insurance, businesses — and yet, three years after the patriarch or matriarch passed, the wealth was gone.

Not because the assets disappeared.

Because the *knowledge* did.

Money is easy to inherit.

Wisdom is not.

Without knowledge, money becomes a magnifier of confusion.

With knowledge, even modest resources can create generational freedom.

That's why I call **financial literacy the missing inheritance.**

THE THREE GENERATIONS RULE

Studies show that 90% of wealth is lost by the third generation.

Here's how it usually happens:

1. **First Generation** earns it — through struggle and sacrifice.

2. **Second Generation** spends it — trying to enjoy what their parents built.

3. **Third Generation** forgets it — having never learned how it was made or why it mattered.

That cycle continues until someone breaks it through education, structure, and values.

You are that someone.

The Money Guardian™ mindset exists to end that pattern — for good.

WHY SCHOOLS DON'T TEACH THIS

Let's be honest:

Our school systems were built for the industrial age — to create employees, not entrepreneurs.

We learn photosynthesis, algebra, and Shakespeare, but not how to read a pay stub, build a business, or structure a trust.

The wealthy aren't born with secret intelligence — they're just educated differently.

They learn money early, often around the dinner table, not from a textbook.

That's what we're about to recreate in your family.

TRANSFORMING YOUR FAMILY INTO A FINANCIAL TEAM

A trust is not just a document; it's a classroom.

Your family becomes the students — and you, the first teacher.

Here's how to build a culture of financial literacy in your household:

1. Hold Monthly Family Money Meetings

Treat your family like a boardroom.

Review income, expenses, goals, and upcoming projects.

Celebrate wins — debt paid off, new investments, charitable giving.

Assign each person a role, even if symbolic:

Role	Function
Trustee-in-Training	Learns oversight and responsibility
Budget Captain	Tracks spending and savings
Investment Analyst	Researches opportunities
Philanthropy Lead	Oversees family giving or charity work

Children who grow up involved in this way learn to respect, not resent, money.

2. Teach Financial Principles by Age Band

You don't need to wait until they're grown to start.

Here's an example structure that I've seen work for families across income levels:

Age	Lesson	Method
6–9	The value of earning	Give small paid tasks and explain savings
10–13	Saving and spending	Open a youth account and track interest
14–16	Income and taxes	Explain W-2 vs 1099 and let them file a mock return
17–21	Investing and credit	Introduce index funds, compound interest, credit scores
22+	Business and trusts	Teach entity ownership, tax planning, and estate design

Each stage builds confidence and curiosity.

3. Create a Family Trust Curriculum

You can turn your Blueprint Trust™ into a lifelong classroom.

Start with a binder (physical or digital) that includes:

- The trust document and structure chart

- Letters of Wishes and Legacy Letters (more in Chapter 11)

- A family mission statement

- Financial goals by generation

- Reading list and training schedule

Once per year, review and update it with your family.

This process transforms the trust from a legal formality into a living institution.

THE BLUEPRINT EDUCATION FRAMEWORK

When I launched **Trust University**, I noticed that most people weren't failing because they lacked opportunity — they failed because they lacked understanding.

Here's the framework I teach my clients:

1. **Exposure** → Learn what exists (trusts, taxes, structure).

2. **Understanding** → See how it applies to you personally.

3. **Execution** → Implement one concept at a time.

4. **Teaching** → Pass it on to someone else.

If you stop at exposure, knowledge evaporates.

If you move to teaching, it multiplies.

That's how you build a family of wealth *guardians*, not just heirs.

CASE STUDY: THE RIVERA FAMILY

The Rivera family came to me with a successful trucking business.

The father, Arturo, was self-made, but his two teenage sons couldn't tell you what a profit-and-loss statement was.

We set up a Blueprint Trust for the business and added a family learning system.

Each quarter, the sons attended "board meetings," learning the difference between income and cash flow, and between assets and liabilities.

By age twenty-one, one son ran the logistics division, and the other managed accounting.

The family not only preserved the business — they expanded it into a new generation.

Knowledge became inheritance.

THE ROLE OF FAITH AND VALUES

Financial literacy without values is empty.

That's why I encourage every family to anchor their trust education in something deeper — purpose, service, and gratitude.

Include faith or moral principles in your financial training.

Remind your family: *Money is a tool, not an idol.*

When wealth is guided by wisdom, it serves humanity, not the other way around.

THE FAMILY MONEY LIBRARY

Start your own small "financial library" at home — a shelf, a folder, a shared drive.

Include foundational books and resources, such as:

- *The Richest Man in Babylon* — George S. Clason
- *Rich Dad Poor Dad* — Robert Kiyosaki
- *The Millionaire Next Door* — Thomas J. Stanley

- *Tax-Free Wealth* — Tom Wheelwright

- Your own trust documents and training notes

Assign one book each quarter and discuss it at your family meetings.

Let your children see you learning too.

MENTORSHIP AND APPRENTICESHIP

At some point, education must become *experience*.

If you own a business, bring your children into the operation — even if it's just observation at first.

Let them see the decisions, the discipline, and the sacrifice.

If you don't own a business, create projects together:

Start a small family investment account, manage a rental, or volunteer as a family in a nonprofit.

The goal is exposure — turning theory into practice.

THE MONEY GUARDIAN™ EDUCATION PLAN

Before moving to the next chapter, build your family's first *Knowledge Plan*:

1. **Schedule** monthly money meetings.

2. **Assign roles** — trustee-in-training, budget captain, philanthropy lead.

3. **Create** a Family Trust Binder or digital drive.

4. **Read** one financial book per quarter.

5. **Host** an annual "Wealth Weekend" — review assets, teach lessons, celebrate progress.

Do this consistently, and your children won't just inherit wealth — they'll inherit mastery.

SUMMARY — KNOWLEDGE IS THE REAL COMPOUND INTEREST

- Money fades; wisdom multiplies.

- Financial literacy breaks generational curses.

- A family that learns together, grows together.

- The Blueprint Trust becomes your family's financial classroom.

- True inheritance is internal — discipline, purpose, and stewardship.

You've learned how to protect and grow wealth.

Now you've learned how to *teach it*.

In the next chapter, we'll move from education to *legacy* — turning your knowledge into a system that endures for generations.

6 — Legacy & Succession: Building What Outlives You

"A good man leaves an inheritance to his children's children."
— Proverbs 13:22 (KJV)

THE TRUE MEASURE OF WEALTH

When I ask clients what they want their legacy to be, most pause.

They think about money, maybe property, maybe a business.

But legacy isn't just what you *leave behind* — it's what continues to live through others after you're gone.

Legacy is architecture.

It's building something designed to stand without you.

And that requires more than income or investments — it requires intention.

INHERITANCE VS. LEGACY

There's a major difference between *inheritance* and *legacy*:

Inheritance	Legacy
What you leave *for* someone	What you leave *in* someone
Transfer of assets	Transfer of wisdom and purpose
Can be spent	Continues to multiply
Ends with death	Begins with death

Inheritance without legacy is like handing someone the keys to a car without ever teaching them how to drive.

Your job as a Money Guardian™ is to make sure they know *both*: how to manage, protect, and multiply what you've built — and why it matters.

WHY LEGACY MUST BE ENGINEERED

Most people think legacy happens automatically.

They assume a will is enough, or that their children "will figure it out."

That's not a plan — that's a gamble.

Legacy must be *engineered* just like a business or a trust:

- With structure

- With process

- With clarity

- With communication

If you fail to define it, the world will define it for you — through courts, taxes, and confusion.

THE PROBLEM WITH WILLS AND PROBATE

I've watched families torn apart because someone relied solely on a will.

A will only tells a probate court what you want; it doesn't avoid court.

Probate is slow, public, and expensive.

- **Average duration:** 6–24 months

- **Average cost:** 5–10% of estate value

- **Public exposure:** Anyone can access your financial details

By contrast, a funded **Blueprint Trust™** avoids probate entirely.

Your assets pass privately, quickly, and according to your instructions — no delays, no arguments, no public record.

That's peace in motion.

SUCCESSION IS LEADERSHIP, NOT PAPERWORK

Succession planning isn't just naming a successor trustee.

It's leadership transfer.

It's asking, *"Who can carry this vision when I can't?"*

Think of your trust as a company and your family as its shareholders.

Succession is choosing and training the next CEO.

Start now by identifying three roles:

1. **Successor Trustee** – The executor of your wishes.

2. **Family Steward** – The relational leader who keeps peace and communication.

3. **Financial Advisor/Strategist** – The technical expert who ensures compliance and growth.

When these three work together, your legacy becomes a system, not a secret.

CASE STUDY: THE ALLEN FAMILY LEGACY

Mr. Allen, a small business owner, once told me, "I don't need a trust. My kids will figure it out."

He passed unexpectedly. The business went into probate, the accounts were frozen, and his three children spent two years in court before receiving anything.

Contrast that with another client, the Porters.

They set up a Blueprint Trust that owned their business, insurance, and real estate.

They trained their eldest daughter as successor trustee and held annual "legacy briefings."

When they passed, the transition took three weeks.

The business never skipped a day.

That's the difference between hope and structure.

THE BLUEPRINT LEGACY FRAMEWORK

Here's the structure I use to help families engineer their legacy:

1. Define the Mission

Ask yourself:

- What values do I want my wealth to express?

- What problems do I want my family to keep solving?

- What kind of people do I want my great-grandchildren to be?

Write this down in a paragraph. It becomes the "why" behind your trust.

2. Fund the Vision

A trust without funding is just paper.

Transfer ownership of your real estate, business entities, life insurance, and key accounts into the trust.

Ensure your insurance payouts go *to the trust,* not individuals.

3. Document the Wisdom

Include **Letters of Wishes** and **Legacy Letters** (see Chapter 11) — personal writings that tell your family how to live the mission, not just manage the money.

4. Train the Next Generation

Host quarterly Family Trust Meetings. Review assets, goals, and roles.

By the time your children inherit leadership, they'll already be living it.

BUILDING A LIVING LEGACY

Legacy doesn't start after death — it starts now.

Use your Blueprint Trust to give while you live:

- Fund education for your grandchildren.

- Support your church or charitable causes.

- Sponsor young entrepreneurs.

- Create family scholarships.

- Invest in community development through the trust.

These acts build *living legacy* — impact you can witness while you're here.

THE ROLE OF FAITH IN LEGACY

I believe legacy without faith is fragile.

Whether your foundation is spiritual, moral, or philosophical, it must have meaning beyond money.

I often tell my clients:

"If your legacy can be measured only in dollars, it's too small."

Anchor your trust's purpose in something that transcends currency — your beliefs, your story, your calling.

That's what turns financial inheritance into generational influence.

PREPARING FOR THE INEVITABLE

Here's the hard truth: everyone reading this will one day exit.

The question is not *if* — but *how prepared will your family be when it happens?*

Succession planning is not morbid. It's responsible.

It's the final act of love — ensuring your family can move forward in order and unity.

I encourage every trust creator to hold what I call a **Legacy Conversation**:

- Sit your family down.

- Explain the trust structure in plain language.

- Share your vision and reasoning.

- Answer their questions.

This conversation eliminates 90% of the confusion that destroys inheritance later.

THE MONEY GUARDIAN™ LEGACY PLAN

Before moving forward, complete your personal Legacy Plan:

1. **Define** your family mission statement.

2. **Select** your successor trustee and financial steward.

3. **Fund** your trust with real assets (titles, deeds, policies).

4. **Write** your Letter of Wishes and Legacy Letter.

5. **Host** your first family Legacy Conversation.

Legacy is not automatic. It's authored.

SUMMARY — WHAT OUTLIVES YOU

- Legacy is built on purpose, not possessions.

- Succession is leadership transfer, not legal paperwork.

- A funded trust ensures peace and privacy.

- Living legacy begins now — give while you're alive.

- Faith and values are the blueprint that money alone can't replace.

When your trust is structured, funded, and guided by wisdom, you don't just leave wealth — you leave direction.

In the next chapter, we'll explore how to take your structure and turn it into **economic empowerment**, where your trust becomes a living engine for freedom and opportunity.

7 — Economic Empowerment Through Structure

"It's not about how much money you make. It's about how your money moves." — Michael A. Carney

WHY STRUCTURE IS THE REAL WEALTH

Economic empowerment doesn't begin with a paycheck.

It begins with *positioning*.

You can earn six figures and still feel broke if your income has no structure.

You can build a business and still be vulnerable if it's all in your name.

You can even own assets and still lose them — if they're not properly protected.

The secret that separates the wealthy from the overworked isn't harder labor — it's smarter structure.

Most people focus on **income creation**.

The wealthy focus on **income control**.

WHAT IS ECONOMIC EMPOWERMENT?

True economic empowerment is more than financial literacy — it's financial *architecture*.

It means:

- You control how and where your money flows.

- You decide when and how it's taxed.

- You legally protect income before it ever reaches your name.

- You turn every dollar into an employee of your vision.

That's what the Blueprint Trust™ was designed to do — shift power from the IRS, creditors, and courts back to *you*.

WHY MOST PEOPLE STAY STUCK

Most Americans operate inside the wrong system.

They are:

- **Employees**, trading time for money taxed at the highest rate

- **Consumers**, not producers

- **Unstructured**, meaning every dollar flows through personal accounts

- **Unprotected**, meaning every asset is exposed

Meanwhile, the wealthy use *the exact same tax code* — they just use it differently.

They don't evade taxes. They engineer them.

When you learn to structure your income through trusts, corporations, and insurance, you start to play the same game.

STRUCTURE IS THE NEW STRATEGY

Here's the truth the financial world doesn't advertise:

"If you control the entity, you control the outcome."

Entities — like LLCs, S-Corps, C-Corps, and trusts — aren't just legal paperwork.

They're *containers* that determine how your money is taxed, used, and transferred.

Let's look at the difference.

Structure Type	Description	Tax Impact	Risk Exposure
Individual (Sole Proprietor)	All income in your name	Highest tax rate	Unlimited liability
LLC (Single-Member)	Legal separation, flexible taxation	Medium	Limited liability
S-Corp	Pass-through with salary/dividend split	Lowered self-employment tax	Corporate protection
C-Corp	Separate taxpayer, strong deductions	Flat tax rate (21%)	Strong protection, complex
Blueprint Trust™	Owns the entity, income flows privately	Strategic tax mitigation	Maximum privacy and protection

When your Blueprint Trust *owns* the business entity, you no longer "make money personally" — your structure does.

THE POWER OF OWNERSHIP TRANSFER

John D. Rockefeller once said, *"Own nothing, control everything."*

He wasn't hiding money — he was protecting it through structure.

By assigning ownership of your business, real estate, and investments to your **Blueprint Trust**, you create *legal distance* between yourself and your wealth.

That distance does three things:

1. **Protects assets** from lawsuits, judgments, and divorce

2. **Reduces taxes** by shifting income into trust and entity structures

3. **Creates generational control** — your family inherits systems, not chaos

You're no longer reacting to money. You're *directing* it.

CASE STUDY: THE STRUCTURED CONTRACTOR

Marcus, a self-employed contractor, made $280,000 a year but paid nearly $90,000 in taxes.

He operated as a sole proprietor, with tools, vehicles, and contracts all under his personal name.

We helped him form:

- A **Construction LLC**, owned by his **Blueprint Trust**
- The LLC elected to be taxed as an **S-Corp**
- The trust became the sole shareholder

Result:

- Marcus paid himself a $70,000 salary (taxed normally)
- The remaining profit ($210,000) flowed to the trust
- The trust invested in real estate and an IUL policy
- His tax burden dropped by 40%
- His liability dropped to zero

He didn't make more money. He just made it move smarter.

THE FLOW OF EMPOWERED MONEY

Let's break down the **Blueprint Money Flow™** — the system the wealthy use, now made accessible to everyone:

1. **Revenue** enters your **business entity** (LLC, S-Corp, etc.).

2. The **entity pays expenses** — marketing, payroll, insurance, etc.

3. **Profit flows** from the entity into your **Blueprint Trust™**.

4. The **trust invests or distributes** money per your rules — to you, your family, or your legacy goals.

5. The **trust owns assets** like real estate, insurance policies, or intellectual property.

Each dollar travels through a legal and tax-optimized system — protected, purposeful, and compounding.

THE ECONOMIC SHIFT:
EMPLOYEE → OWNER → TRUST

Most people live on one level of the wealth pyramid — the **employee level**.

Level	Role	Taxed As	Leverage
Employee	Works for others	W-2 (highest rate)	None
Self-Employed	Works for self	1099 (high rate)	Limited
Business Owner	Money works for you	1120S/1120	Moderate
Trust Owner	Entity owns assets	1041	High leverage

Economic empowerment means climbing that pyramid — and the Blueprint Trust is your elevator.

HOW STRUCTURE CREATES FREEDOM

Freedom isn't doing whatever you want — it's being *free from unnecessary control*.

When your wealth is structured:

- You choose *how* income is taxed.

- You choose *when* income is distributed.

- You choose *who* benefits and *how long* it lasts.

You are no longer a tax subject — you are a tax architect.

And the best part? You don't have to be rich to start.

You become rich *because* you start.

BLUEPRINT EMPOWERMENT FLOW MAP

Here's a simplified version of how to build your empowerment structure:

1. **Form an Entity** — Start with an LLC or S-Corp for your business or side income.

2. **Establish a Blueprint Trust** — This will own your entity and receive profits.

3. **Assign Ownership** — Retitle key assets under the trust (properties, vehicles, IP).

4. **Set Up a Trust Bank Account** — Separate from your personal finances.

5. **Create an IUL Policy** — Owned by the trust for tax-free growth and protection.

6. **Flow Income Strategically** — Pay yourself, fund the trust, and reinvest intentionally.

7. **Review Quarterly** — Meet with your CPA or strategist to refine deductions and timing.

Follow this map, and you'll build not just a structure — but a system that multiplies.

ECONOMIC EMPOWERMENT FOR FAMILIES AND COMMUNITIES

This chapter isn't just about individual gain — it's about restoring power to families and communities that have been financially excluded for generations.

Economic oppression thrives where education and access are missing.

The Blueprint Trust democratizes both.

When one family establishes a trust, they don't just protect their assets — they create a *blueprint* that others can follow.

Imagine communities where:

- Parents teach children to be trustees, not just heirs

- Churches own property through trusts

- Entrepreneurs operate tax-smart, protected businesses

- Wealth circulates internally instead of leaking out through taxation and litigation

That's not a dream — it's strategy.

FAITH, PURPOSE, AND EMPOWERMENT

Wealth without purpose is just accumulation.

But when structure aligns with faith and values, money becomes a tool for mission.

That's why I remind my clients:

> "Economic empowerment is stewardship. You're not hoarding wealth — you're preserving it for impact."

The Blueprint Trust allows you to give with confidence, invest with integrity, and build a financial kingdom that reflects your values.

THE MONEY GUARDIAN™ EMPOWERMENT PLAN

Before moving to the next chapter, complete your Empowerment Plan:

1. **Identify your current structure** — Are you an employee, self-employed, or entity-based?

2. **Establish your Blueprint Trust™** — Draft and fund it properly.

3. **Transfer ownership** of your income streams and key assets.

4. **Reclassify your income** — Shift from personal to entity-based earnings.

5. **Implement tax strategies** — Use deductions, distributions, and IULs strategically.

6. **Educate your family** — Host your first family empowerment meeting.

You are no longer a financial passenger. You're the architect.

SUMMARY — THE POWER OF STRUCTURE

- Structure determines freedom.

- Entities and trusts are the foundation of wealth control.

- Empowerment isn't income — it's strategy.

- The Blueprint Trust makes generational control accessible to everyone.

- You don't need to be rich to use the system — you use the system to become rich.

The difference between the middle class and the wealthy isn't the amount of money they earn — it's how their money *moves*.

In the next chapter, we'll go deeper into that movement — into the heart of your trust's leadership: **the role of the trustee**.

8 — The Role of the Trustee: The Guardian of the Guardian

"The trust is the body. The trustee is the heartbeat." — Michael A. Carney

WHY THE TRUSTEE MATTERS MORE THAN YOU THINK

A trust is only as strong as the person — or team — managing it.

You can build the perfect structure, write airtight language, and craft your legacy plan to perfection... but if the wrong trustee takes over, your masterpiece can collapse in months.

The **trustee** is the engine of your Blueprint Trust™.

They hold fiduciary power — meaning, under law, they must act in the best interests of the beneficiaries and follow the trust's written instructions to the letter.

But they also hold something deeper: your *intent*.

They become the voice of your vision once you're gone.

When I teach clients about trustees, I always say:

> "The trustee is not just the manager of money — they are the guardian of meaning."

WHAT EXACTLY IS A TRUSTEE?

A **trustee** is the legal steward of your trust.

They're responsible for executing your instructions, managing assets, paying bills, filing taxes, and distributing funds to beneficiaries according to your wishes.

In simpler terms: they keep your plan alive when you no longer can.

Every trust has:

- **A Grantor** — the person who creates and funds it (you).

- **A Trustee** — the person or entity that manages it.

- **Beneficiaries** — the people who benefit from it (your family, charity, etc.).

The trustee holds legal title to the trust's assets.

But they don't own them. They manage them for others — and that distinction matters.

THE FIDUCIARY STANDARD: SACRED DUTY, NOT SUGGESTION

The trustee has the highest duty recognized by law: the *fiduciary duty*.

That means they must:

1. **Act in Good Faith** — No self-dealing, favoritism, or neglect.

2. **Follow the Trust's Terms** — Exactly as written, unless legally impossible.

3. **Be Loyal to the Beneficiaries** — Their needs come before personal gain.

4. **Preserve and Grow the Assets** — The trust should not stagnate.

5. **Keep Records and Report Transparently** — Annual statements, taxes, and logs.

Violating this duty can result in removal, fines, or even legal liability.

That's why the trustee role should be approached with *serious reverence*.

THE TRUSTEE'S CORE RESPONSIBILITIES

Here's what a competent trustee actually does on a day-to-day and annual basis:

1. Asset Management

- Oversees real estate, business interests, bank accounts, and investments.

- Ensures bills, insurance, and taxes are paid.

- Maintains property and ensures proper titling.

2. Distribution Control

- Makes payments or distributions to beneficiaries based on the rules of the trust.

- Withholds or delays distributions if conditions aren't met (for discretionary trusts).

3. Recordkeeping and Accounting

- Keeps receipts, ledgers, and statements.

- Prepares annual reports for beneficiaries.

- Files the trust's tax return (Form 1041).

4. Tax Coordination

- Works with accountants and financial advisors to minimize trust-level taxes.

- Issues K-1s to beneficiaries when necessary.

5. Legacy Administration

- Executes the emotional and spiritual side — carrying out Letters of Wishes or Legacy Letters.

- Communicates with family members to maintain order and alignment.

In short: The trustee is the CEO of your legacy.

CHOOSING THE RIGHT TRUSTEE

Selecting your trustee might be one of the most important financial decisions you ever make.

Don't choose based on emotion or seniority.

Choose based on competence, character, and commitment.

Ask these questions:

- Does this person understand money — or have access to people who do?
- Can they handle family conflict without collapsing under pressure?
- Will they honor my instructions even if they disagree?
- Are they organized, ethical, and stable?
- Will they outlive me — or can they pass the baton effectively?

If even one of those answers is uncertain, you may need a *professional trustee.*

TYPES OF TRUSTEES

1. Individual Trustee

Usually a family member or friend.

Pros: Knows your family personally, flexible, lower cost.

Cons: May lack financial expertise or neutrality.

2. Co-Trustees

Two or more people share responsibilities.

Pros: Balance of emotional and financial oversight.

Cons: Can lead to disputes or delays if not clearly defined.

3. Corporate or Professional Trustee

A law firm, CPA, or trust management company.

> Pros: Professional oversight, objectivity, longevity.

> Cons: More formal, annual fees apply.

Hybrid Option:

A family member + professional co-trustee = heart + expertise.

This is the most balanced model for complex family trusts.

TRAINING THE TRUSTEE: LEGACY BRIEFINGS

Don't just *name* your trustee — *train* them.

Hold what I call a **Legacy Briefing** once a year.

Invite your successor trustee(s) to review:

- The trust binder (official copy + digital backup)

- Property titles, account information, and insurance policies

- IUL performance summaries and investment reports

- Letters of Wishes and family mission statements

These meetings keep your legacy alive and your successor prepared.

It's easier to carry your vision when they've already heard it from your voice.

CASE STUDY: THE PREPARED SUCCESSOR

Elaine, a retired nurse, named her oldest son, Jordan, as her successor trustee.

Each year, she held a 90-minute family "Legacy Lunch."

She'd update her children on her trust, her assets, and any new instructions.

When Elaine passed unexpectedly, Jordan stepped in seamlessly.

He knew the passwords, contacts, and next steps.

Probate was avoided. Bills were paid. Distributions were clear.

Her family grieved — but they didn't scramble.

That's the power of preparation.

THE TRUSTEE'S EMOTIONAL ROLE

A trustee doesn't just manage money — they manage emotions.

They must be calm under pressure, compassionate yet firm, and committed to peace.

When family disputes arise, the trustee becomes the anchor — the voice of reason that points everyone back to the trust document.

That's why your trust should be crystal clear, leaving no room for confusion or manipulation.

"Clarity is kindness. Ambiguity is chaos."

If you don't make your wishes plain, you put your family in conflict.

A well-written trust removes the guesswork — and protects the relationships that matter most.

HOW TO EQUIP A TRUSTEE FOR SUCCESS

Provide a "Trustee Toolkit" that includes:

- The complete trust document

- Copies of deeds, policies, and titles

- Contact list for all advisors
  (CPA, attorney, insurance agent)

- Summary sheet of assets and account numbers

- Letter of Wishes

- Annual tax instructions (Form 1041 guidance)

Give them professional partners.

A trustee doesn't need to be an expert — they need access to experts.

Surround them with a **Trust Team:**

- Attorney

- CPA

- Financial advisor

- Insurance specialist

- Family mediator or counselor (optional)

COMPENSATING THE TRUSTEE

Paying your trustee isn't greedy — it's responsible.

Managing a trust takes time, effort, and liability.

Your trust should clearly define compensation terms.

Common options:

- **Flat annual fee** (for simple trusts)

- **Percentage of trust income or assets**
  (industry standard: 1–2%)

- **Hourly rate** for specific duties

- **Waived compensation** (for family members, by choice)

The key is *clarity and fairness.*

Your trustee deserves compensation for safeguarding your family's future.

WHEN TRUSTEES FAIL

Even with the best intentions, trustees can fail.

They might:

- Mismanage funds or commingle accounts

- Ignore their reporting obligations

- Favor one beneficiary over another

- Refuse to act or communicate

When this happens, your trust should include **removal clauses** — allowing beneficiaries, co-trustees, or advisors to replace them.

Power should never concentrate in one unchecked hand.

That's why the Blueprint Trust includes *successor tiers* — ensuring continuity no matter what happens.

REAL-WORLD CAUTIONARY TALE

A client once came to me devastated.

Her father had left behind a $2 million trust — but her aunt, the trustee, refused to distribute funds.

The aunt claimed "it wasn't time yet," but in reality, she didn't understand the accounting or the legal obligations.

After a year of legal wrangling, the family lost nearly $80,000 in attorney fees.

All because the original trust lacked trustee oversight clauses.

That's why your Blueprint Trust builds checks and balances *into the DNA* of the document.

THE TRUSTEE VS. EXECUTOR

These two roles are often confused.

Role	Oversees	Works Through	Duration
Executor	Your will and estate	Probate court	Short-term (until estate is closed)
Trustee	Your trust and legacy	Privately, outside court	Long-term (years or decades)

Think of it this way:

- The executor closes your book.

- The trustee continues your story.

That's why every Blueprint Trust includes a **pour-over will**, ensuring any leftover assets outside the trust are transferred in seamlessly.

THE TRUSTEE READINESS BLUEPRINT™

Here's your checklist to ensure your trustee is fully equipped to carry your vision forward:

- Identify your ideal trustee (integrity, competence, availability).

- Name at least one successor trustee — or a professional backup.

- Draft compensation terms within the trust document.

- Create a physical + digital trust binder.

- Host annual Legacy Briefings with your successor.

- Document your Letter of Wishes and Legacy Letter.

- Include trustee removal and replacement clauses.

- Build a professional advisory team around your trustee.

When you complete this checklist, your trust becomes more than a document — it becomes a living institution.

SUMMARY — THE GUARDIAN OF THE GUARDIAN

The trust is your protector.

The trustee is its guardian.

Choose wisely.

Train deliberately.

Equip generously.

A trust without a capable trustee is a car without an engine — beautiful, but motionless.

A trained trustee ensures your mission doesn't die with you.

And when that happens — when your family, your business, and your purpose all move forward seamlessly — you'll have built not just a trust, but a *dynasty*.

9 — Tax Strategy for Entrepreneurs and High Earners

"The tax code isn't your enemy — it's your instruction manual." — Michael A. Carney

WHY MOST PEOPLE LOSE THE TAX GAME

Taxes are the single largest expense most people will ever pay.

Bigger than their mortgage.

Bigger than their children's education.

And for entrepreneurs and high earners, the loss is magnified — not because they make too much, but because they structure too little.

Most taxpayers are playing checkers while the wealthy are playing chess.

The difference? The wealthy understand one simple truth:

The IRS doesn't reward the hardest worker — it rewards the smartest planner.

If you're tired of watching your income disappear into taxes while others legally keep and grow theirs, this chapter is your turning point.

THE THREE LAYERS OF STRATEGIC TAX ARCHITECTURE

Every powerful tax plan — especially one built into a **Blueprint Trust™** — functions on three layers:

1. **Entity Selection & Structure** — How your business is classified and taxed

2. **Asset Ownership & Flow** — Where income lands and who owns it

3. **Trust-Level Optimization** — How the trust itself manages and minimizes tax liability

Let's break each one down.

Layer 1: Entity Selection & Structure

Choosing the right entity is the foundation of tax leverage.

Entity Type	Pros	Cons	Tax Filing
Sole Proprietor	Simple to set up	100% liability and highest tax bracket	Schedule C
LLC (Disregarded)	Liability protection	Still taxed as individual unless reclassified	Schedule C or 1065
S-Corporation	Avoids double taxation, self-employment tax savings	Requires payroll compliance	1120S
C-Corporation	21% flat rate, strong benefits and deductions	Double taxation if not structured under a trust	1120

Now, when your **Blueprint Trust™ owns the entity,** everything changes.

The business's profits can flow up to the trust instead of to you personally.

You can draw a reasonable salary (taxed normally) while the trust retains profits for reinvestment or growth — taxed strategically at the trust level.

That's where the second layer begins.

Layer 2: Asset Ownership & Flow

Ownership determines taxation.

When your trust owns the business, the property, and even the insurance, you've shifted from **taxpayer** to **trust architect.**

Here's the Blueprint Flow:

1. **Income** → earned by your business (LLC/S-Corp).

2. **Expenses** → business pays operating costs (deductible).

3. **Net Profit** → flows to your **Blueprint Trust™** as a distribution.

4. **The Trust** → reinvests, purchases assets, funds insurance, or supports family education.

5. **You (as Trustee)** → control distributions and reinvestments per the trust terms.

The key advantage is that the trust now *legally* owns the profit, allowing you to manage income recognition, distribution timing, and tax classification.

LAYER 3: TRUST-LEVEL OPTIMIZATION

Now the fun begins.

The trust becomes its own taxpayer under IRS rules (Form 1041).

But it's *strategically designed* to reduce or defer taxes.

Under **IRC §§641–685**, a properly structured non-grantor trust can:

- Deduct distributions made to beneficiaries

- Pass income to beneficiaries in lower tax brackets

- Retain income when strategic to do so

- Classify income differently
  (capital gains vs. ordinary income)

- Offset taxes with charitable contributions or
  insurance funding

When used with professional accounting and compliance, the trust becomes a **tax management vehicle** — not a tax avoidance tool.

UNDERSTANDING "RECLASSIFICATION OF INCOME"

Most entrepreneurs make money as individuals — which means every dollar earned is taxed up to 37% plus self-employment tax.

With the **Blueprint Trust structure**, income can be reclassified into different tax categories:

- **Wages** — taxed as ordinary income

- **Distributions** — taxed once (and sometimes deferred)

- **Capital Gains** — lower rate

- **Dividends** — preferential rates
- **Trust Income** — deductible when distributed strategically

You're using the same laws Fortune 500 companies and wealthy families have used for decades — legally and transparently.

CASE STUDY 1: THE CONSULTANT WHO RECLAIMED $40,000

Name: Danielle

Income: $220,000 (consulting)

Problem: Paying over $70,000 per year in taxes

Danielle formed an LLC taxed as an S-Corp and assigned ownership to her **Blueprint Trust.**

She paid herself a $65,000 salary and flowed the rest to the trust as profit.

The trust:

- Funded an Indexed Universal Life (IUL) policy
- Purchased real estate
- Claimed deductions for education and administrative costs

Outcome:

- Reduced taxable income by 40%
- Amended prior returns and received $18,000 in IRS refunds + interest

- Built a trust-owned IUL now worth $60,000 in cash value

"For the first time, I felt like the system was working for me — not against me."

CASE STUDY 2: THE REAL ESTATE COUPLE WHO AVOIDED CATASTROPHE

Names: Carlos & Elena

Portfolio: 4 rental properties

Problem: Tenant lawsuit threatened their net worth

Their properties were retitled into LLCs — each owned by their **Blueprint Trust™**.

When the lawsuit hit, the claim stopped at the LLC layer — their personal names were nowhere on the deeds.

Their trust:

- Retained property income

- Paid for repairs and taxes

- Distributed net income to heirs tax-efficiently

Outcome:

- Lawsuit dismissed — no personal exposure

- Properties avoided probate

- Income flowed through trust with optimized taxation

  "We went from panic to peace in a matter of weeks. It's like we were playing the wrong game all these years."

THE IRS OWES YOU — WITH INTEREST

Yes, you read that right.

When you amend old tax returns to correct overpayments or restructure under a new entity/trust system, the IRS must pay interest on any refund owed.

Under **IRC §6611,** the interest accrues from the date the overpayment was made until the refund is issued.

One of my clients recovered over $12,000 — not in tax savings, but in **IRS interest payments.**

This isn't a loophole. It's law.

That's why the Blueprint Trust process includes a **3-year tax amendment review** — to reclaim what you've already overpaid.

INTEGRATING THE IUL: THE TRIPLE TAX SHIELD

An **Indexed Universal Life (IUL)** policy, when owned by your Blueprint Trust™, becomes a multi-purpose financial powerhouse.

Here's how:

1. **Growth** — Cash value grows tax-deferred, indexed to market performance.

2. **Access** — You can borrow from it tax-free while it continues to compound.

3. **Transfer** — The death benefit passes to the trust tax-free (IRC §101).

By combining trust ownership with IUL growth, you build perpetual, tax-free compounding — what I call *The Triple Shield.*

Income taxes are deferred.

Capital gains are minimized.

Estate taxes are eliminated.

The wealthy have done this for decades. The Blueprint Trust just makes it accessible for everyone.

BLUEPRINT EXAMPLE: THE $300,000 INCOME PLAY

Let's visualize it:

Business Income: $300,000 (LLC owned by Blueprint Trust)

- $60,000 salary paid to you

- $240,000 profit flows to trust

- Trust funds $30,000 into IUL

- $50,000 reinvested into real estate

- $25,000 distribution to child for education

- $135,000 retained for trust growth

Personal Taxable Income: Only $60,000

Wealth Controlled: $300,000+

Probate Exposure: $0

This is not avoidance. It's design.

You're simply moving your wealth through a smarter system.

CHARITABLE INTEGRATION

Under **IRC §642(c)**, trusts can deduct charitable donations made directly from trust income.

That means your giving can reduce your taxable liability while advancing your mission.

When you designate giving through your trust — to a church, scholarship fund, or foundation — you create **tax-deductible impact.**

Philanthropy and strategy don't have to compete. They can complement each other.

AUDIT-PROOF COMPLIANCE

The Blueprint Trust doesn't hide income — it organizes it.

Every flow is recorded, every account documented.

When structured properly, your trust becomes the cleanest audit trail the IRS could ever ask for.

Transparency is power.

If you can prove where the money goes, you can legally decide *how much stays.*

THE MONEY GUARDIAN™ TAX PLAYBOOK

To build your own tax architecture, follow these steps:

1. **Entity Audit:**

   Review your business structure with a CPA. Reclassify to S-Corp or LLC taxed as S if needed.

2. **Blueprint Trust Setup:**

Form and fund your trust. Assign ownership of your entity to it.

3. **Income Flow Redesign:**

Route profit through the trust instead of personal accounts.

4. **IUL Integration:**

Use trust funds to purchase IUL for tax-free compounding.

5. **Charitable Strategy:**

Direct trust income to a Donor-Advised Fund or charitable beneficiary for deductions.

6. **Amend Prior Returns:**

Audit the last 3 years for overpayments. File amended returns if eligible.

7. **Quarterly Optimization:**

Revisit your structure every 90 days with your tax strategist. Adjust timing, distributions, and reinvestments.

SUMMARY — PLAY THE GAME TO WIN

You don't have to be a CPA to win the tax game — you just need to know the rules.

The wealthy don't cheat. They *read the manual.*

Every deduction, classification, and trust strategy is already written into law.

The Blueprint Trust simply connects those laws into one elegant, ethical system.

Remember:

- Taxes are not punishment — they're policy.

- You don't owe more than what's required by law.

- The IRS rewards structure, not struggle.

By the end of this chapter, you're no longer a taxpayer.

You're a **Tax Architect** — a Money Guardian™ who plays to win.

10 — Case Studies: Real-World Application of the Blueprint Trust™

"Knowledge becomes wisdom when it's lived." — Michael A. Carney

WHY REAL STORIES MATTER

Reading about trusts and tax codes is one thing.

Watching them change real lives — that's something else entirely.

The following case studies are based on true scenarios I've personally encountered while guiding clients through the **Blueprint Trust™ System**. Names and details have been changed for privacy, but the lessons are one-hundred percent real.

Each person came in with a story: confusion, fear, frustration.

Each left with clarity, confidence, and control.

Let's see how it happens.

CASE STUDY 1: DANIELLE T. —
THE OVER-TAXED CONSULTANT

Background

Danielle was a 42-year-old business strategist earning $215,000 a year.

Despite her success, she dreaded tax season — every April brought another $70,000 bill.

Her CPA's advice? *"You just make too much. That's the price of success."*

Problem

Danielle filed as a sole proprietor.

Every dollar she earned was taxed at the highest rate, and she had no legal separation between herself and her business.

No asset protection. No leverage. No growth strategy.

The Blueprint Solution

We formed an **LLC** for Danielle's consulting firm and had her **Blueprint Trust™** become the sole member.

She began paying herself a modest $60,000 salary and directing the remaining profits to her trust.

The trust then:

- Funded an **Indexed Universal Life (IUL)** policy for tax-free growth

- Paid legitimate business expenses through her entity

- Allocated funds to education for her two sons

- Filed its own Form 1041, shifting taxable income out of her personal bracket

Outcome

- Tax burden reduced by **$45,000 in year one**

- Recovered **$28,000 in prior-year refunds + interest**

- Built **$60,000 cash value** inside her IUL

- Created a documented legacy plan for her children

Lesson Learned:

You don't have to earn less — you have to *own smarter*.

CASE STUDY 2: CARLOS & ELENA M. — THE LANDLORDS FACING A LAWSUIT

Background

Carlos and Elena owned four rental properties across Ohio.

They'd worked for decades to build equity and were finally enjoying steady income.

Until one rainy afternoon when a tenant slipped on a walkway and sued them for $750,000.

Problem

All properties were titled in their personal names.

That meant their savings, cars, and even retirement accounts were exposed.

The Blueprint Solution

We established a **Blueprint Trust™** and created separate **LLCs** for each property.

The trust became the member-owner of all four LLCs.

We added an umbrella insurance policy inside the trust and retitled every deed.

Outcome

- The lawsuit was absorbed at the LLC level — their personal assets untouched

- Properties continued generating income during litigation

- Rental income now flows through the trust tax-efficiently

- Children designated as successor beneficiaries

Lesson Learned:

Liability doesn't knock before it enters — structure is your door lock.

CASE STUDY 3: LAVERNE J. — THE WIDOWED TEACHER TURNED INVESTOR

Background

At 61, Laverne lived modestly on a teacher's pension and a small rental property.

After her husband's death, she wanted to ensure her grandchildren would be cared for — but probate terrified her.

Problem

Her assets were scattered: a checking account, one property, two insurance policies.

No trust, no coordination, and no plan for who would manage anything after she passed.

The Blueprint Solution

We built her **Blueprint Trust™** and transferred ownership of:

- Her home and rental property deeds

- Bank accounts and life-insurance policies

- A new **final-expense plan** owned by the trust

She wrote a **Legacy Letter** — a heartfelt message to her grandkids, sharing her values and life lessons.

Outcome

- Probate avoided entirely

- Her trust now holds all assets privately

- Insurance pays directly to the trust for grandchildren's benefit

- Legacy Letter stored with the documents for future reading

Lesson Learned:

Legacy isn't about millions — it's about *intention*.

CASE STUDY 4: MARCUS D. — THE OVERWORKED CONTRACTOR

Background

Marcus was a 39-year-old contractor grossing $280,000 a year.

Despite long hours, his take-home pay was shrinking.

Taxes, equipment loans, and lawsuits kept him on the edge.

Problem

Marcus operated as a sole proprietor.

His trucks, tools, and contracts were all in his personal name.

One jobsite injury claim nearly bankrupted him.

The Blueprint Solution

We formed a **Construction LLC**, owned by his **Blueprint Trust™**.

Marcus became the manager — not the owner — of the business.

The trust purchased:

- Liability insurance

- Vehicles

- Equipment through leasing arrangements

It also funded an **IUL** policy and acquired a small rental duplex.

Outcome

- Tax liability cut by 38 percent

- Lawsuit dismissed (LLC absorbed exposure)

- Rental income and IUL loans now funding expansion
- Marcus's family protected by clear succession plan

Lesson Learned:

You don't need another contract — you need a *container*.

CASE STUDY 5: THE JOHNSON FAMILY — THE FIRST-GENERATION DYNASTY

Background

Brian and Latasha Johnson were first-generation wealth builders.

Together they earned $320,000 from a trucking company and real-estate flips.

They wanted to leave something lasting for their three children but had no coordinated system.

The Blueprint Solution

We established a **Blueprint Family Trust™**, with both spouses as co-trustees.

Their trucking company became trust-owned; profits funded a **trust bank account** that paid for:

- Life insurance premiums
- College savings
- Family travel (documented as educational experiences)

They began holding quarterly **Family Board Meetings** — teaching their children how moncy flows through the structure.

Outcome

Family net worth grew 30 percent in 18 months

Taxes dropped significantly

Children learned financial literacy firsthand

Lesson Learned:

Generational wealth starts when the *first generation documents it.*

CASE STUDY 6: THE CHURCH THAT BUILT ITS OWN LEGACY

Background

A small congregation in Texas was losing members and struggling to maintain its building.

They relied on weekly donations — until one lawsuit over a parking-lot injury threatened to shut them down.

Problem

The church owned the property in its corporate name, with no legal separation from leadership.

The Blueprint Solution

We formed a **Faith-Based Blueprint Trust™**.

The trust became the owner of the property, equipment, and accounts.

A separate operating nonprofit leased assets from the trust.

Outcome

- Lawsuit absorbed by the operating entity — the property untouched

- Members began contributing to a trust-owned charitable IUL

- The church now funds scholarships and community projects tax-efficiently

Lesson Learned:

Even ministries need money management that matches their mission.

CASE STUDY 7: THE ATHLETE WHO PLANNED AHEAD

Background

Jamal, a 27-year-old professional basketball player, was earning $3.2 million a year.

He wanted to protect his wealth from lawsuits, taxes, and misman-agement — before the headlines hit.

The Blueprint Solution

We structured his endorsement company under a **Blueprint Trust™.**

Salaries, bonuses, and brand deals flowed through an S-Corp owned by the trust.

The trust funded an IUL, purchased real estate, and created a charitable foundation.

Outcome

- Assets legally separated from personal liability

- $400,000 in annual tax savings

- Estate plan completed before age 30

- Foundation now funds youth mentorship programs nationwide

Lesson Learned:

Wealth without structure is temporary fame. Structure turns it into generational impact.

BLUEPRINT REFLECTION — FIND YOUR STORY

You've just seen how the Blueprint Trust transforms:

- Taxes into tools

- Liability into leverage

- Income into inheritance

These people aren't anomalies. They're examples of what happens when strategy meets intention.

Every story begins the same way:

Someone gets tired of watching their money leak away.

They decide to learn. They decide to structure.

And then — everything changes.

YOUR TURN: THE MONEY GUARDIAN™ CHALLENGE

1. **Identify Your Risk:** What's currently in your name that shouldn't be?

2. **Audit Your Taxes:** Where are you overpaying or under-structuring?

3. **Blueprint Your Flow:** Map your income path — from entity → trust → legacy.

4. **Educate Your Heirs:** Start your first family meeting this month.

5. **Document Your Vision:** Write your Letter of Wishes or Legacy Letter.

Your story belongs in the next edition of this book.

All it takes is a decision — today.

11 — Letters of Wishes & Legacy Letters: Passing Down Your Voice

"When your words outlive you, your influence never dies." — Michael A. Carney

WHY MONEY ALONE ISN'T ENOUGH

You can leave behind assets, real estate, insurance policies, and investments —but if your family doesn't know **who you were, what you stood for**, or **why you built it**, your wealth won't last.

In fact, studies show that **90% of inherited wealth is gone by the third generation.**

Not because of bad luck — but because of lost instruction.

That's why the **Letters of Wishes** and **Legacy Letters** exist.

They are the bridge between your paperwork and your purpose.

THE POWER OF THE WRITTEN WORD

When a family loses a loved one, the pain comes not just from absence, but from silence.

They wonder:

- What would Mom have wanted me to do?

- How would Dad have handled this decision?

- Did they forgive me?

- Were they proud of me?

Your **Legacy Letter** answers those questions long after you're gone.

It lets your family *hear your voice, feel your heart,* and *understand your values* — even in your absence.

It's not a legal document. It's a love document.

And it belongs at the center of your Blueprint Trust™.

THE LETTER OF WISHES — THE PRIVATE COMPASS FOR YOUR TRUSTEE

A **Letter of Wishes** is a confidential, non-legally-binding letter that sits alongside your trust.

It's written to your **trustee**, not your beneficiaries.

Think of it as your "how-to guide" for administering your legacy with grace, wisdom, and discretion.

It tells the trustee:

- *How* to distribute funds

- *When* to pause or delay a distribution

- *What* values or behaviors should guide their decisions

- *Who* to support and in what manner

- *Why* you set things up the way you did

EXAMPLE TOPICS TO INCLUDE:

- Guidance for helping children start a business or buy a home

- Support for higher education, mentorship, or trade training

- Conditions for responsible financial behavior (e.g., sobriety, employment, giving)

- Handling of family property (keep or sell)

- Support for aging parents or special-needs dependents

- Spiritual guidance or faith-based preferences

This letter gives your trustee human context — the "why" behind your wealth plan.

It ensures your money isn't just managed, but *ministered.*

THE LEGACY LETTER — SPEAKING TO THE HEART OF GENERATIONS

If the **Letter of Wishes** speaks to the *head*, the **Legacy Letter** speaks to the *heart.*

This is your chance to tell your story.

To pass on not just *what* you built, but *who* you became.

You can write it as a letter, a series of journal entries, or even a recorded video message stored digitally in your trust binder.

A LEGACY LETTER CAN INCLUDE:

- Your faith and spiritual journey

- The principles you lived by

- The sacrifices that built your success

- Words of encouragement to your children and grandchildren

- Your greatest lessons, regrets, and hopes

- Family stories or defining memories

- Instructions for how you want them to love, give, and lead

SAMPLE LEGACY LETTER OPENING

My beloved family,

If you are reading this, it means I've gone home — but not far.

I want you to know that everything I built, everything I saved, and everything I taught was never about money.

It was about freedom — the freedom to choose your own path, to protect your family, and to make an impact.

Use what I've left not as a cushion, but as a compass.

Love each other. Forgive quickly. Stay humble.

Keep God first, keep your name clean, and keep our legacy growing.

With all my heart,

— Dad

HOW TO WRITE YOUR OWN LEGACY LETTER

Don't overthink it. You don't need perfect grammar or poetic words — just honesty.

Here's a step-by-step guide:

1. **Start with Gratitude** — Acknowledge your loved ones and thank them for being part of your journey.

2. **Tell Your Story** — Where you came from, what shaped you, and what you overcame.

3. **Share Your Values** — The principles you lived by and want carried forward.

4. **Give Guidance** — How to use the trust's resources wisely.

5. **Speak to the Future** — Share your hopes, dreams, and blessings for generations yet to come.

6. **End with Love** — Leave them with comfort and encouragement.

You can update it at any time — every five years, or whenever life changes meaningfully.

PRESERVING AND STORING YOUR LETTERS

Both letters should live securely within your **Trust Binder** and digital archives.

Here's the proper placement:

Document	Purpose	Stored With
The Trust	Legal control	Original trust binder + digital backup
Letter of Wishes	Trustee guidance	Sealed, private with attorney or corporate trustee
Legacy Letter	Message to family	Copy in trust binder + digital cloud backup
Video Message (optional)	Emotional legacy	Secure digital vault or encrypted drive

You can also choose to seal your Legacy Letter in an envelope with instructions:

> "Open only after my passing" or "To be read at the family meeting."

It creates a sacred moment — one of healing and clarity, not confusion.

THE POWER OF THE FAMILY READING

One of the most healing moments I've ever witnessed was during a trust administration.

A father, a Vietnam veteran, had left a Legacy Letter to be read aloud by his trustee at the first family meeting after his passing.

His words brought laughter, tears, and peace.

He apologized for things left unsaid.

He blessed each child by name.

He reminded them to stay united and to keep the family business thriving.

That single letter prevented years of bitterness.

It brought direction where there could have been division.

That's the miracle of a Legacy Letter.

FAITH AND THE ETERNAL BLUEPRINT

Scripture says,

> *"My people are destroyed for lack of knowledge."*
> — Hosea 4:6 (KJV)

Your Legacy Letter ensures your descendants are not destroyed by ignorance — financial, emotional, or spiritual.

It's your opportunity to write a generational epistle, one that will guide your heirs through both prosperity and pressure.

You are not just leaving money — you are leaving *meaning*.

THE MONEY GUARDIAN™ LEGACY COMMUNICATION PLAN

Use this simple checklist to complete your Legacy Communication System:

- Write your **Letter of Wishes** (trustee guidance)

- Write your **Legacy Letter** (family message)

- Record a **Video Legacy** (optional but powerful)

- Store all copies in your **Trust Binder** and secure digital backup

- Schedule a **Family Meeting** to discuss your vision while you're alive

- Update every 5 years or upon major life changes

- Inform your trustee and successor where to find all documents

Your voice is the compass that keeps your family aligned when you're no longer here to lead them in person.

SUMMARY — YOUR WORDS ARE WEALTH

Money fades. Markets change. But your words — your story — last forever.

A **Letter of Wishes** gives your trustee wisdom.

A **Legacy Letter** gives your family love.

Together, they complete the Blueprint Trust™ — turning your plan from a stack of documents into a living, breathing legacy.

You are the author of your family's future.

And with your words, you will be heard for generations.

12 — Building a Family Office with Your Trust: Turning Legacy into an Institution

"A wealthy family without structure will lose everything in three generations. A structured family, even without wealth, will create it within one." — Michael A. Carney

FROM TRUST TO INSTITUTION

You've built awareness.

You've secured protection.

You've established growth.

You've passed on knowledge.

You've anchored legacy.

Now, it's time to **institutionalize it all** — to turn your trust into a *Family Office*.

A Family Office isn't about being rich. It's about being *organized*.

It's the system wealthy families have used for centuries to keep power, purpose, and prosperity alive long after the founder has passed.

When you combine the **Blueprint Trust**™ with a simple yet powerful family governance structure, you no longer have a collection of assets — you have a generational enterprise.

WHAT IS A FAMILY OFFICE, REALLY?

Most people hear "Family Office" and think of billionaires — the Waltons, Rockefellers, or Gates.

They imagine skyscrapers, advisors, and fleets of accountants.

But that's only one version — the *institutional* family office.

The Blueprint version — what we'll call your **Blueprint Family Office**™ **(BFO)** — is scalable, accessible, and completely customizable to your level of wealth.

It's not about size. It's about **structure**.

At its core, a Family Office is a **private, family-run organization** that manages:

- Wealth preservation
- Tax strategy
- Asset growth and allocation
- Estate planning and legal oversight
- Philanthropy and giving
- Family education and communication
- Generational continuity

In simple terms:

> It's how you make sure the system you built doesn't die when you do.

THE BLUEPRINT FAMILY OFFICE™ FOUNDATION

At the center of your Family Office is the **Blueprint Trust™**.

Everything flows through it. Everything reports back to it. Everything is protected by it.

Below the trust, you layer the entities, roles, and systems that make the structure run.

Here's how the hierarchy looks:

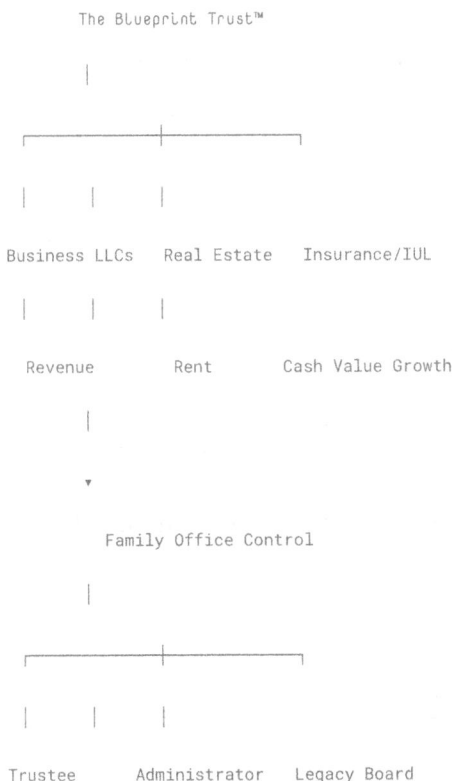

```
                    The Blueprint Trust™
                            |
            ┌───────────────┴───────────────┐
            |           |           |
      Business LLCs   Real Estate   Insurance/IUL
            |           |           |
        Revenue        Rent      Cash Value Growth
            |
            ▼
               Family Office Control
                        |
            ┌───────────┴───────────┐
            |           |           |
         Trustee    Administrator   Legacy Board
```

This isn't complexity — it's clarity.

Every dollar, decision, and document has a home and a handler.

THE FIVE PILLARS OF THE BLUEPRINT FAMILY OFFICE™

Your Family Office isn't just a filing system — it's a living organism built on five pillars:

1. **Governance** – Defines leadership, rules, and meeting systems.

2. **Finance & Tax** – Manages income, investments, and compliance.

3. **Education** – Trains heirs to be stewards, not spenders.

4. **Philanthropy** – Directs giving and community impact.

5. **Legacy & Continuity** – Preserves values, stories, and succession.

Each pillar is vital. Together, they create harmony.

PILLAR 1: GOVERNANCE — THE STRUCTURE OF STEWARDSHIP

Without leadership, wealth becomes chaos.

Governance defines **who makes decisions**, **how often**, and **under what principles**.

Role	Purpose
Trustee	Oversees the trust, ensures rules are followed, manages distributions
Administrator	Handles day-to-day paperwork, communication, and banking
Legacy Coordinator	Leads education, mentorship, and generational development
Financial Steward	Manages investments, budgeting, and tax coordination
Family Council Chair	Leads meetings, ensures family unity and communication

KEY ROLES:

You can fill these roles with family members, advisors, or professionals — or blend both.

The key is clarity and accountability.

THE FAMILY CONSTITUTION

Your Family Constitution is the document that defines:

- Core values and mission

- Decision-making rules

- Conflict resolution process

- Succession policies

- Education requirements for heirs

It's not a legal document, but it's one of the most powerful instruments of family unity.

When signed and read annually, it keeps everyone aligned with the founder's vision.

PILLAR 2: FINANCE & TAX —
THE ENGINE OF PERPETUAL GROWTH

A Family Office is, at its heart, a financial control center.

Its goal is to make sure that every dollar in your ecosystem has a job and a direction.

FUNCTIONS OF THE FINANCIAL PILLAR:

- Maintain trust accounting
  (Form 1041 and beneficiary K-1s)

- Track cash flow across entities

- Review insurance and IUL performance

- Conduct annual tax audits and adjustments

- Manage investments through a unified lens

THE POWER OF CENTRALIZATION

Instead of each family member managing their own accounts, everything flows through the trust.

This allows for:

- Unified financial reporting

- Better tax efficiency

- Consolidated purchasing and investing power

- Reduced risk through centralized control

The goal is to operate like a private family bank — efficient, compliant, and coordinated.

PILLAR 3: EDUCATION — TRAINING THE NEXT GENERATION

The greatest threat to wealth isn't taxes or inflation — it's ignorance.

That's why education is built into your Family Office from day one.

THE FAMILY ACADEMY MODEL

Set up your own *Family Academy* — a quarterly workshop or weekend gathering focused on:

- Understanding how the trust works
- Learning financial literacy fundamentals
- Reviewing investments and business operations
- Teaching stewardship, generosity, and ethics

Each generation should graduate from "beneficiary" to "steward."

CURRICULUM IDEAS BY AGE:

Age	Focus	Tools
8–12	Money basics & saving	Jars, apps, family games
13–17	Earning, budgeting, investing	Mock portfolios, allowance systems
18–25	Credit, taxes, entrepreneurship	Online courses, internships
25+	Trust operations & leadership	Trustee shadowing, financial meetings

Your family doesn't need a school system.

You *are* the school system.

PILLAR 4: PHILANTHROPY — TURNING WEALTH INTO WORSHIP

True wealth is stewardship — not ownership.

A well-run Family Office uses philanthropy as a teaching tool.

Your trust can fund:

- **Donor-Advised Funds (DAFs)** for tax-advantaged giving

- **Scholarships** in your family name

- **Community investments** — housing, small businesses, churches

- **Annual giving budgets** — where children propose causes they care about

This pillar ensures the family stays mission-driven, not money-driven.

"Giving keeps greed from taking root."

PILLAR 5: LEGACY & CONTINUITY — IMMORTALITY THROUGH INTENTION

Legacy is what binds your system together.

It ensures that the vision outlives the visionary.

Your Family Office should have a **Legacy Continuity Plan**, which includes:

- Updated trust and estate documents

- Successor trustee training

- Annual "State of the Family Office" reports

- Archiving of Legacy Letters, family videos, and stories

- Business succession plans and buy-sell agreements

Each of these ensures that if something happens to you tomorrow, your system doesn't collapse — it activates.

HOSTING YOUR FIRST FAMILY OFFICE MEETING

Your first Family Office meeting will set the tone for generations.

Sample Agenda:

1. Opening Prayer or Mission Statement

2. Review of the Family Constitution

3. Overview of Trust and Asset Performance

4. Education Segment (Financial Literacy Topic)

5. Philanthropy Review (Donations or Projects)

6. Upcoming Events, Birthdays, and Projects

7. Closing Words or Legacy Reading

Keep it simple, structured, and sacred.

These meetings will become a cherished tradition — a reminder that your family is not just a group of people, but a purpose.

HOW TO ESTABLISH YOUR
BLUEPRINT FAMILY OFFICE™

Here's a simple, step-by-step roadmap:

1. **Create Your Blueprint Trust™** – Ensure it's properly executed and funded.

2. **Form Supporting Entities** – LLCs, corporations, or partnerships under the trust.

3. **Appoint Key Roles** – Trustees, administrators, and stewards.

4. **Draft Your Family Constitution** – Outline values and governance.

5. **Establish Your Family Office Account** – Centralized banking for trust and entities.

6. **Launch Your Family Meetings** – Quarterly at minimum.

7. **Document Everything** – Keep trust binders updated, with copies stored securely.

8. **Educate and Empower** – Train your heirs while you're alive.

9. **Integrate Philanthropy** – Build giving into the DNA of your trust.

10. **Review Annually** – Adjust, evolve, and pass down leadership intentionally.

You don't need millions to start.

You just need structure, commitment, and communication.

THE MULTI-GENERATIONAL VISION

Your trust can live for 100 years or more.

Your family office ensures it stays active, relevant, and effective through every generation.

Each generation adds new:

- Assets

- Letters

- Lessons

- Leaders

It's a living ecosystem — one that expands while staying rooted in the founder's mission.

FAITH AND THE FINAL WORD

Everything in this book — every chapter, every principle — is built on this truth:

> *"A good man leaveth an inheritance to his children's children."* — Proverbs 13:22

But inheritance isn't just money.

It's mindset. It's management. It's mission.

When you institutionalize your wealth through the **Blueprint Family Office™,** you are creating a *covenant* — a promise that your family's prosperity will never again be accidental.

You've become what few ever do — not just a provider, but a **Money Guardian™**.

A leader who doesn't just build income, but engineers immortality.

SUMMARY — THE BLUEPRINT COMPLETED

Let's recap the journey:

1. **Awareness** — You saw where you were.

2. **Protection** — You built your shield.

3. **Growth** — You ignited compounding.

4. **Knowledge** — You taught the next generation.

5. **Legacy** — You designed your forever plan.

6. **Family Office** — You institutionalized it all.

Now, your name is no longer just a memory.

It's a *movement*.

Your trust is no longer just a document.

It's a *dynasty*.

And your story — your faith, your wisdom, your work — will echo through generations as proof that one person's discipline can rewrite a family's destiny.

> *"Your legacy isn't what you leave behind.*
> *It's what you build while you're here — and who*
> *you build it for."— Michael A. Carney*

About the Author – Michael A. Carney

Michael A. Carney is a visionary in the world of financial literacy, tax mitigation, and trust-based estate planning. As the Founder and CEO of Acuracounts, Inc., he has dedicated his career to helping individuals, families, and business owners protect and multiply their wealth — not through loopholes, but through the legal tools hidden in plain sight.

Born and raised in California, Michael holds a degree in Theology and Business Administration with a concentration in Accounting from California Baptist University. He later studied law at California Southern Law School, where he honed his understanding of the legal frameworks that empower strategic wealth preservation through family trusts, business structuring, and tax planning.

Michael created the Blueprint Trust System™ and launched Trust University, a one-of-a-kind educational platform that demystifies the trust process for everyday families and high-net-worth individuals alike. His mission is to end generational poverty and elevate financial literacy — especially in underserved communities.

Through seminars, speaking engagements, and media appearances, Michael has educated thousands on how to legally safeguard their assets and build legacies that endure.

He is the proud father of three and a strong believer in faith, stewardship, and community empowerment.

"Your legacy isn't just what you leave behind. It's what you build while you're here — and who you build it for."

—Michael A. Carney

www.ingramcontent.com/pod-product-compliance
Lightning Source LLC
Chambersburg PA
CBHW071427210326
41597CB00020B/3684